MATHEMATICS WITH

TEDDY BEARS

By

Elizabeth Graham

illustrated by

Rebecca Hardy and Andrew Fournier

1990 Elizabeth Graham

First Published 1990
Second Impression 1993
Third Impression 1994

Published by
Claire Publications
Unit 8, Tey Brook Craft Centre
Great Tey, Colchester
Essex, CO6 1JE

ISBN   1 871098 09 2

The activities in this book were developed from working with group of children playing with a tub of Teddies.

It was fascinating to watch the mathematics which was being generated as they experimented with the ideas offered , invented their own and set each other tasks and projects. Comments like ' I bet you can't -----' ' Mine is   bigger...' Can you make it go further...?'tumbled from them. They were completely involved in handling the data, measuring, estimating, counting, building, making and working together. Their inventiveness, creativity and persistence was amazing.

As your children work on the ideas offered in this book, new and exciting developments will emerge and a wealth of mathematical activities will follow.

How many Teddies can you
hold in one hand?

Guess, then count.

1. How many Teddies can your friend hold?

2. Will your Teddies line up in 2s?

3. Will your Teddies line up in 3s?

Bet you can't find the smallest number of Teddies that will line up in 2s, 3s and 6s.

How many Teddies can you
hold in both hands?

Guess, then count.

1. How many Teddies can 2 people hold?
   How many can 3 people hold?

2. Find enough people to hold 50 Teddies.

3. How many people are needed to hold 100 Teddies?

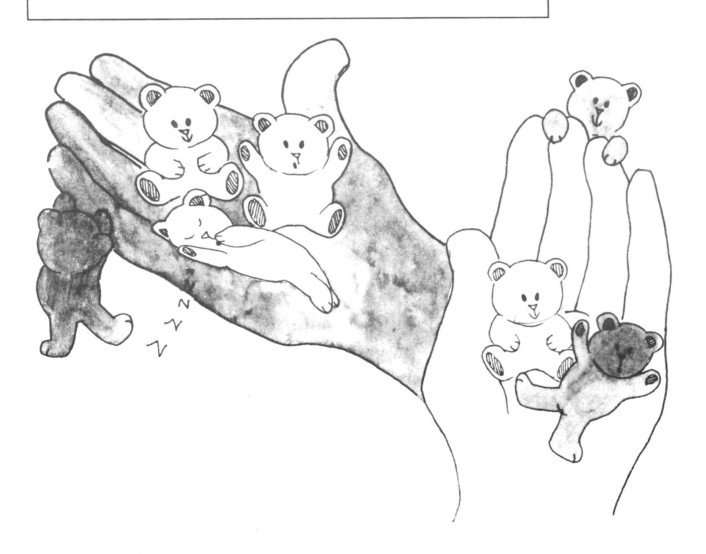

<u>With some friends</u> find out who can hold the most Teddies in their hands.

Make a chart to show the results for the whole class.

Design a certificate for the winner.

How long is your arm?

Measure it with Teddies.

1. Choose 5 friends. Guess how many Teddies will fit along their arms. Now count.

2. Make a chart to show your results.

Bet you can't guess how many Teddies long their strides will be?

Measure their strides.

Were you right?

Make some Teddy cookies.

You need 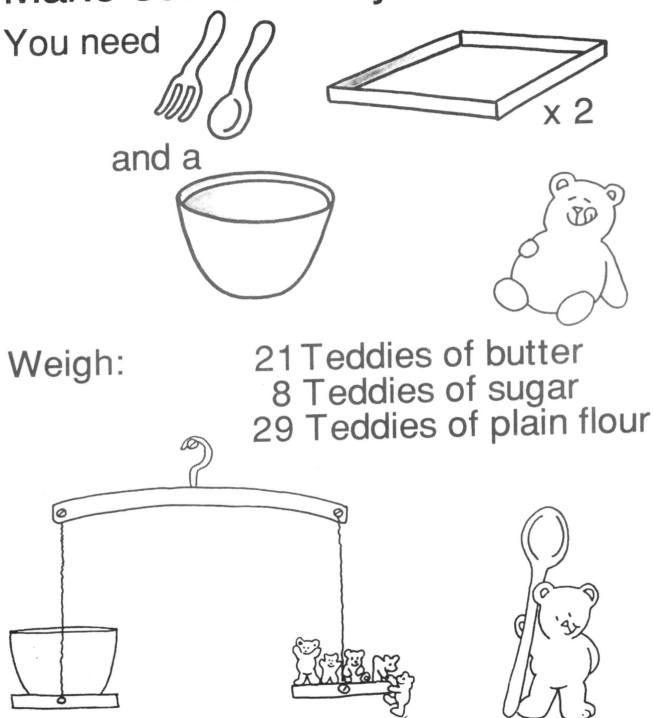 x 2

and a

Weigh: 21 Teddies of butter
         8 Teddies of sugar
        29 Teddies of plain flour

Turn on the cooker to 300°F or 150°C
Grease the baking trays.

1. Cream the butter and suger in bowl until soft.

2. Mix in the <u>sifted</u> flour and **press** into a ball.

3. Roll this out until it is $\frac{1}{2}$ cm thick.

Cut out some
Teddy cookies
with me.

4. Put the Teddy shapes on the baking tray and prick with a fork.

5. Cook for 25 minutes.

<u>Bet you can't</u> wait until
they are cool before you
eat them!

How many Teddies will stand across your chair?

Guess, then count.

Measure with Teddies:-

1. two things which are wider than your chair,

2. one thing narrower than your chair,

3. your table.

<u>Bet you can't</u> find 5 different sized chairs,
then measure them with Teddies.

Make a Teddy ruler.

Cut a piece of paper 10
touching Teddies long.

1. Find 5 things to measure. Use your ruler and your Teddies.

2. Find some things 1 ruler and 5 Teddies long.

3. Find some things 2 rulers and 5 Teddies long.

Bet you can't make a chart to show what you have been doing.

Do page 15 first

You need Teddies and Teddy rulers.
Measure how tall you are in Teddies.

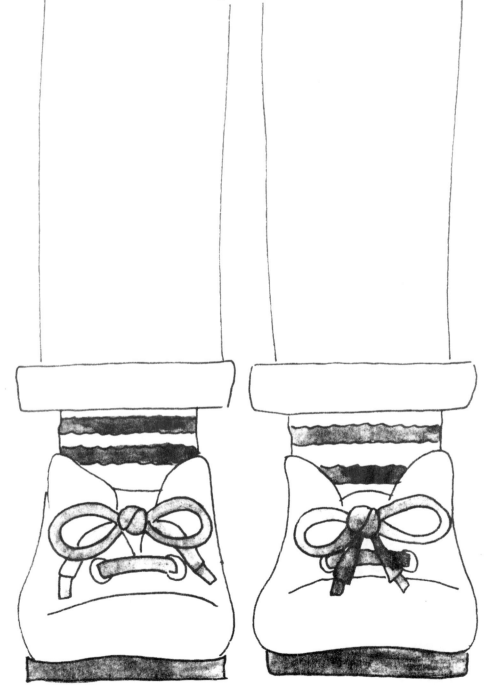

Use Teddies and Teddy rulers:

1. How tall is your **mother**?

2. How tall is your **father**?

3. Your pet? your friend? your teacher?

Bet you can't draw a picture to show your results.

Find a container.

Guess how many Teddies will fit inside it.

Put Teddies in.

Count them.

Use only the Teddies from your container:

1. Find **some** other things that those Teddies will fill.

2. Find or make something that half those Teddies will fill.

3. Find or make something that a quarter of those Teddies will fill

JAM.

Ask a friend to make a container that 50 Teddies would fit into.

You need 30 Teddies and 5 different sized containers.
Put all the Teddies in each one.
What do you notice?

1. Which is the biggest container? How do you know? Put them in order.

2. Make a box just big enough to hold them all.

3. Make a container big enough to hold twice as many.

Bet you can't make a chart to show how you can count the Teddies easily.

Wrap up some Teddies .
Ask a friend to guess how
many Teddies there are.

Were they right?

1. Let your friend wrap up a parcel of Teddies for you to guess.

2. Can you make up some other parcels of Teddies for friends to guess?

3. Record your guesses and find out who was the closest.

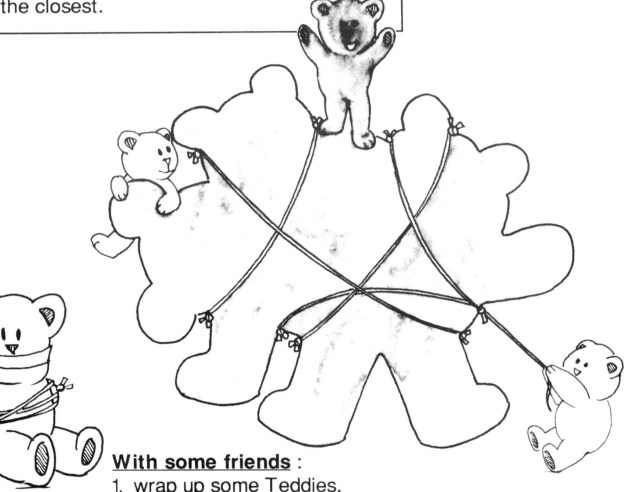

With some friends :

1. wrap up some Teddies,

2. let your friends ask 5 questions about the number,

3. let them guess how many Teddies there are in the parcel.

Fill a container with Teddies.

How much water can you pour in as well?

1. Find a container which holds more Teddies and more water.

2. Find a container which holds the same number of Teddies and more water.

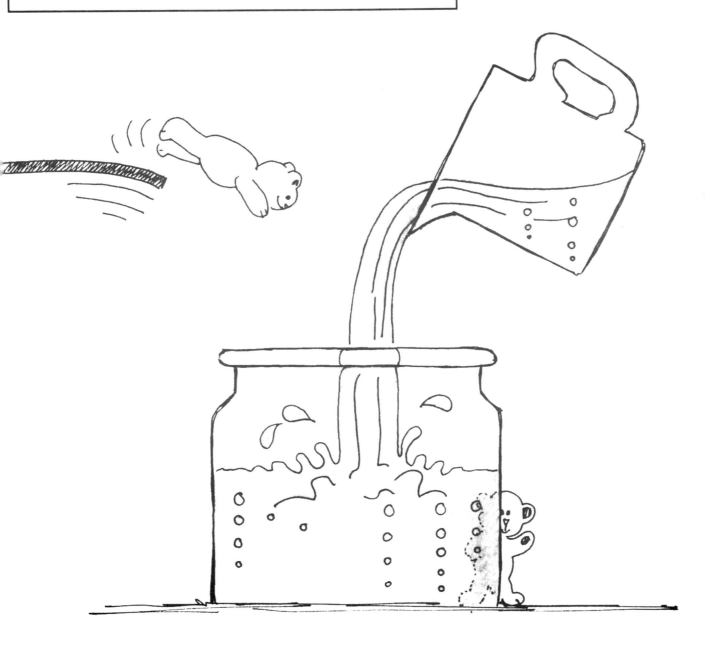

With some friends, find a container which will hold 1 cup of water and 10 Teddies.

Half fill a straight-sided
container with water.
Put a mark at the water level.

Drop some Teddies in.
What happens to the water
level?

1. How many Teddies do you need to make the water rise to the top?

2. Take the Teddies out one at a time. What happens to the water?

3. Draw a picture to show what you have been doing.

Get a straight-sided container:
     drop in 5 Teddies, mark the water level,
     drop in 5 more, mark the water level,
     drop in 5 more, mark the water level.

Can you carry on? What do you notice?

How many Teddies will balance with a small shoe?

Find something else to balance with the same number of Teddies.

1. Find 3 things that will balance with fewer Teddies.

2. Find 3 things that will balance with more Teddies.

3. Draw a picture to show what you have done.

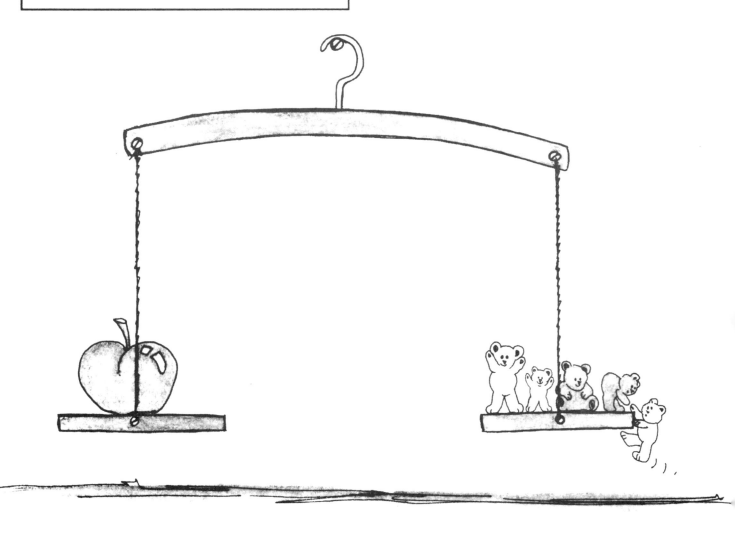

With some friends: choose five small things. Take it in turns to guess how many Teddies will balance them.

Check your guesses.

Record the results.

Draw around your foot.

Fill the outline with Teddies.

Count how many there are.

1. How many Teddies will fit on your friend's footprint?

2. Your teacher's footprint?

3. Do the same with handprints.

4. Record your results.

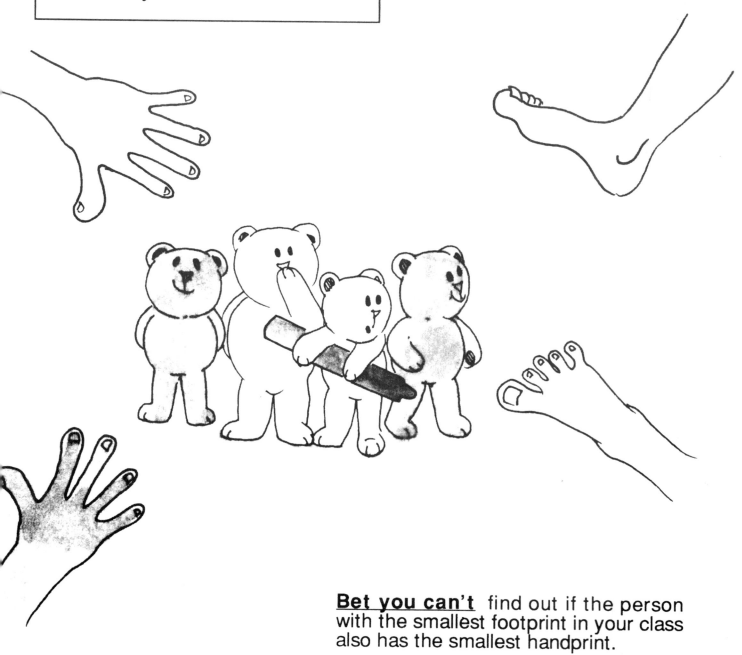

Bet you can't find out if the person with the smallest footprint in your class also has the smallest handprint.

Use Teddies to measure with.

Find the smallest book in the class.

How many Teddies will cover it?

Put Teddies on and count.

1. What else will those Teddies cover?

2. What will 10 Teddies cover?

3. What will 30 Teddies cover?

Bet you can't find something to cover with 100 Teddies.

Draw some shapes that 20 Teddies will fit into.

1. Draw a shape for half the Teddies to stand in.

2. Draw a different shape for the other half to stand in.

3. Draw a shape for a quarter of the Teddies to stand in.

Bet you can't draw 4 different shapes for 100 Teddies to stand in.

Use clay
Make a boat for a Teddy.

1. Make a boat for two Teddies

2. Make a boat for 20 Teddies out of Lego.

3. Have a competition:
   who can build a boat to carry the most Teddies?

Bet you can't make your boat float.

You need boxes or bricks.

Make a car for one Teddy to ride in.

1. Make a car for 2, 3 or 4 Teddies.

2. Can you make your car move?

Bet you can't make a moving bus that will carry 10 Teddies.

You need boxes cubes or bricks.

Make a house for a family of Teddies.

1. Make chairs for the family.

2. Make a table.

3. Make some more furniture for the family.

<u>Bet you can't</u> build a school for Teddies.

Make a slide for a Teddy.

1. How long does a Teddy take to slide to the bottom?

2. Can you make her go faster?

3. Can you make her go more slowly?

Bet you can't make a water slide.

Make a strong swing for a Teddy.

1. Push it once. How many times did it swing?

2. Does it swing longer without Teddies on?

3. Use boxes and string to make a swing for 5 Teddies.

HELP!

Make a moving roundabout for the Teddies.

1. Push it once. How long does it go round for?

2. Does it go for longer with more Teddies on it?

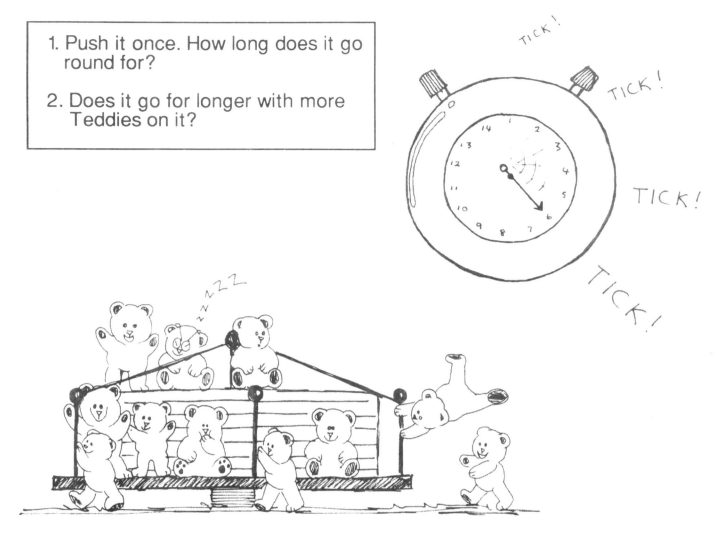

Bet you can't make a Teddy merry-go-round.

Use your swing, slide and roundabout to build a playpark.

Can you build a climbing frame for Teddies.

1. Find places for all the Teddies.

2. What else can you make for the playpark?

<u>Bet you can't</u> make a plan or a map of your playpark.

Make a parachute for a Teddy.

1. Take a Teddy on her own and a Teddy in a parachute.
   Drop them. Which lands first?

2. Drop a Teddy in a parachute from a high place.
   How many times can you clap your hands before she lands?

3. Try again. What else can you do before she stops?

Bet you can't make your parachute for a Teddy so you can clap 10 times before she lands.

Make a Teddy as

BIG as 50 Teddies

TEDDY RULER

50

Draw a colourful chart or picture to show what you have done.

With some friends, find out as many things about Big Teddy as you can.

Using Teddy Bears, measure who has the

biggest

foot!

hand!

nose!

finger!

thumb!

55

1. Show how you measured your hands.

2. Show how you measured your feet.

3. Show how you measured your nose.

Bet you can't make a big picture show all your measurements.

Line up the Teddies like this:

red red blue red red blue.

Carry on the pattern.

What colour is the
10th Teddy?
20th Teddy?

1. Make up your own pattern using red and blue Teddies.

2. Get a friend to continue it .

3. Make a different pattern using green and yellow or yellow and red.

Bet you can't take 7 Teddies and start a pattern using all of them.

Ask a friend to continue it.

You need 3 different coloured
Teddies.
How many ways can you line
them up?

Draw a picture of all the ways.

1. Try with 4 Teddies.

2. Make a table to show your results.

Teddies	Ways
1	1
2	2
3	?
4	?

<u>Bet you can't</u> find out how many ways you can line up 5 Teddies?

Make a chart.

Line up the Teddies like this:

Red blue green red blue green

Carry on the pattern

What colour is
the 10th Teddy?
the 15th Teddy?

1. Make up a pattern which starts with two greens.

2. What colour is the 9th Teddy? 18th Teddy?

3. Can you work out which colour the 27th Teddy would be without making the pattern that long?

GREEN

GREEN

?

RED YELLOW GREEN BLUE

18th

Bet you can't make up a pattern which reads 3.1.2.3.1.2.3.1.2.

9th

Make a pattern where the 20th Teddy is blue.

Make 5 different patterns which fit this rule.

1. Make a pattern where the 10th Teddy is red.

2. Make 5 patterns which fit this rule.

3. Make patterns where the 2nd Teddy is blue and the 6th one is yellow. How many patterns can you make?

Have a go!!

Think up some colour rules like:
        5th Teddy is green
        2nd Teddy is red.
that you could make 20 patterns for.

Can your friends guess the rules by looking at your patterns?